FROM **WAX** TO **CRAYON**

by Robin Nelson

Lerner Publications Company / Minneapolis

Lerner Publications Company
A division of Lerner Publishing Group, Inc.
241 First Avenue North
Minneapolis, MN 55401 U.S.A.

Website address: www.lernerbooks.com

Library of Congress Cataloging-in-Publication Data

Nelson, Robin, 1971–
    From wax to crayon / by Robin Nelson.
        p. cm. — (Start to finish)
    ISBN-13: 978–0–8225–4660–3 (lib. bdg. : alk. paper)
    ISBN-10: 0–8225–4660–4 (lib. bdg. : alk. paper)
    1. Crayons—Juvenile literature. [1. Crayons.] I. Title.
II. Start to finish (Minneapolis, Minn.)
TS1268 .N45 2003
741.2'3—dc21   2002006583

Manufactured in the United States of America
6 – DP – 8/1/11

The photographs in this book appear courtesy of: © PhotoDisc Royalty Free by Getty Images, cover, p. 3; Photos courtesy Binney & Smith Inc., Crayola; the chevron and serpentine designs are registered trademarks; the rainbow/swash is a trademark of Binney & Smith Inc., used with permission, pp. 1 (all), 5, 9, 11, 13, 15, 17, 19, 23; © Todd Strand/Independent Picture Service, p. 7; © Freightliner Corporation, p. 21.

Table of Contents

I color with crayons.

How are they made?

Wax melts.

Crayons start as clear wax. Wax is made into crayons at a **factory**. Large tanks heat the wax. The wax melts into a gooey liquid.

A worker adds color.

Pipes carry the clear wax into many pots called **vats.** A worker adds colored powder called **pigment** to the vats. A different color is stirred into each vat.

The wax is shaped.

The colored wax is poured into a **mold.** The mold has many holes. Each hole is shaped like a crayon. The wax fills the holes.

9

The wax gets hard.

Cold water flows under the mold. It cools the wax. Cooling makes the wax hard. The wax becomes crayons.

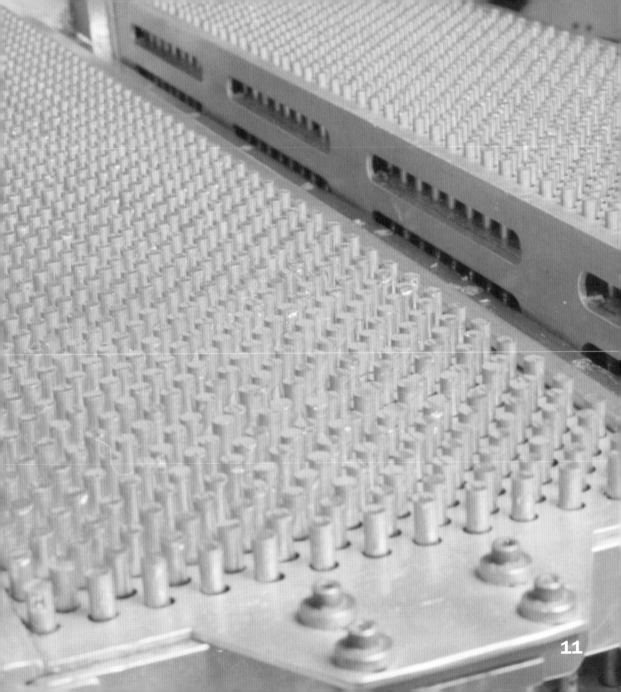

11

A worker checks the crayons.

The crayons are taken out of the mold. A worker checks each crayon for chips or dents. Crayons with chips or dents will be melted and molded again.

A machine wraps the crayons.

The crayons are sent into a machine that spins. It wraps each crayon in a piece of paper. The paper is called a **label.** The label tells the name of the crayon's color.

15

A machine sorts the crayons.

Crayons of the same color line up in the slots of a sorting machine. The machine sorts the crayons into sets. A set has crayons of different colors.

The crayons are boxed.

A packing machine puts the sets into boxes. Some boxes have just a few crayons. Some boxes have crayons of every color the factory makes.

The crayons are sent to stores.

A worker fills large cartons with boxes of crayons. The cartons are packed onto a truck. The truck takes the crayons to stores.

I draw pictures with many colors!

People buy crayons at the store.
My crayon box has many colors.
What should I draw?

Glossary

factory (FAK-tuh-ree): a building where things are made

label (LAY-buhl): a paper that names a crayon's color

mold (MOHLD): a container that shapes crayons

pigment (PIHG-mehnt): a powder that colors wax

vats (VATS): pots for melting wax

Index